THE SEARCH

by CAROL LYNN PEARSON

Illustrated by Trevor Southey

Doubleday & Company, Inc.
Garden City, New York

ISBN: 0-385-07758-0
Library of Congress Catalog Card Number 74-028895
Copyright © 1970 by Carol Lynn Pearson
All Rights Reserved
Printed in the United States of America
9 8 7 6 5 4

*And he that seeketh
findeth.*

TABLE OF CONTENTS

THE SOURCE

If God is love,
The source,
The spring,
Should not the lover
Pilgrimage there —
Reverently
Seeking supply? —

That the cup he gives
Will not be dry.

UNFED

We feed one another
In rations,
Serve affection
Measured to
The minimum daily
Requirement,
The very acceptable
Least —

While love
Bursts the walls
Of our larder,
Wondering,
Amazed,
Why we are afraid
To feast.

THE VOW

How could I hide you
From hate?
I would,
Though my arms break
With the trying.

Life leans in
At the window there,
With its bag
Of dark treasures
Trying for your eyes —
So utterly open,
So unaware.

You will see
Men smile over blood,
And you will know
There is hate.
You may see bombs
And butcheries,
And you will know
There is horror.

Against all this
What can I do?
Only vow
That before you
Leave my arms,
You will know
Past ever doubting
That there is
Love, too.

THE PATH

A day came
For getting somewhere
Before dark.
I looked down a path,
Beginning in good stones
And leading a lovely
Buttercupped way —
To a bog.

Too bad,
I thought,
That a traveler
May not
Choose half a path,
Discarding
The destination.
Perhaps
A brief stroll
Until the rocks give?

No.
This was a day
For getting somewhere
Before dark.
And the sun
Does not slow
To let one go
The safe part,
And then —
Walk the same stones
Back
And start again.

ON THE DIVINE
SCHOOL SYSTEM

I've
Unnumbered eons
For learning
To govern a world,
A galaxy —

But just
Seventy years
For the harder course —
Governing me.

LAMENT
OF A GROUCH

I knew
That in heaven
All are happy.
But I wish
I'd known
The reason
Before:

Only
To the happy
Do they
Open the door.

PREJUDICE

The celestial soul —
Bigger than boundaries —
Extends himself
Past labels of name,
Or place, or shade.

It will take,
I think,
A long time
To learn how.

Should we not
Start now?

THE SCHOLAR

He knew Abraham,
Isaac and Jacob
Like a fellow
Tent-dweller.
He had chronicled
Their lives,
Their very thoughts.

And he knew
His own son
Like the stranger
Who is given shelter
For the night
And bread
To help him on
His lost way.

He knew tears,
Finally, too,
Bitter and burning —
When he saw how
Huge a stewardship
He had traded
For a pot of
Learning.

THE UNWRITTEN POEM

Sometimes —
In a sitting down moment
On a day
Of stove-heating the sad-irons
And layering newspaper between
Quilts to keep us warmer —
I heard my mother say,
"I wish I had time
To write a poem."
And then she would start
The potatoes.

When I was twelve
A thing happened that
Broke my heart —
A school thing I've forgotten now.
For hours I cried my humiliation
Into a handkerchief.

Next day my mother
Brought it in from ironing —
That handkerchief —
And gave it to me special.
"Here," she laid it in my lap.
"You've had it in happy times
And in sad.
There'll be more of both.
Keep it, and it will remind you
The better follows the bad."

She went back to ironing,
And my fingers traced
The little flowers of fading blue.

I can remember other poems
She left me, too.

THE FRIEND

Let me
Be the hearth
Where you sit
To work your clay.
I'll not say
"Shape it like this,
Or like that,"
I promise.

Let me watch
As you
In absolute agency
Mold your
Mortal dream.

Only —
Sit close
And let me give
A little light,
A little warmth.
Yes —
Warmth especially.

Cold clay yields
To no form.
Let me
Be your hearth.
Sit close —
Be warm.

THE PRUNING

It was time
To prune the apricots.
"Only one bud
Every few inches of tree
Or they won't grow,"
Said my father.

I didn't believe him,
Though,
And I kept one branch
All full of flowers,
For I knew
That come fall
They would all
Be beautiful and bright
And big —
Ever so big.

Early one morning
In fruit time
I ran to the orchard,
And beneath
The heavy-hanging
Golden crop
I harvested my apricots,
My many, many,
Tiny apricots.

When it was dark
I fed them
To the cow.

I prune now.

NEW CHILD

I savor
This mutual feast:

You
At my breast,
Desperately
Drinking life —

And me
Watching,
Touching,
Sipping eagerly
On your sweet
Evidence
Of immortality.

RETURN TO A CHILDHOOD STREAM

When I last
Walked here,
I was one —
Singular as
The small wet stone
That cools my palm.
I was one —
Like the lone leaf
Floating calm
In the water-whirl.

When I last
Walked here,
I was one —
A girl.

But in life's
Brief burgeoning,
I walk today
A trinity:
Here in this body —
The man,
The child,
And me.

NEEDED

The earth needs
Only nature.
If spring follows
Snow,
If new seeds
Swell —
Earth will go
On and on,
Content.

I have watched
With folded hands,
An uneasy guest.

But now —
Suddenly
I am nature.
And I am needed
As all tomorrow's
Orchards
Need the present
Tree.

How good —
This nine-month
Indispensability.

FIRST INCREASE

Now,
Lying breathless
On the meridian
Of eternity,
I slowly gather
Vision
And view God
With a new
Familiarity.

From the beginning
We have been bound
As child and Father.
But here —
In this brief
Earth-moment —
I have found
His gift of Godhood,
Given His gift
Of life.

A double miracle
Dawned this morn:
A baby breathed,
And too,
The God in me
Was born.

MOTHER TO CHILD

Look —
Your little fist
Fits mine
Like the pit
In a plum.

I think,
In the time
Before remembering,
These two hands
Clasped companionably,
Then parted.

Help me, child.
Forgive me
When I fail you.
I'm your mother,
True,
But in the end
Merely an older equal
Doing her faltering best
For a dear
Small friend.

THE WEANING

There is cloth now
Between you
And my breast —
Cloth
And a little pain.

This is the
Beginning.
I take your face
In my hands
And guide your gaze
Away, out there —
To the fruit trees,
To the stars.

My arms,
Though empty,
Fold comfort
To a mother-heart
That yearns for nursing,
Yet knows that weaning
Is the bigger part.

THE WOMAN

God fashioned me
For feeding,
And set me in
A hungry land.

I give —
To satisfy
The unconscious appetite
Of the unborn,
And the child's
First thirsting need.

I give —
To be
Sweet sustenance
To aching man,
And then
Quiet comfort
To a weary, wanting
World.

There is much
Hunger here.

Oh,
Father — fill me,
That I may nourish
Generously.

TO AN ADOPTED

I
Did not plant you,
True.
But when
The season is done —
When the alternate
Prayers for sun
And for rain
Are counted —
When the pain
Of weeding
And the pride
Of watching
Are through —

Then
I will hold you
High,
A shining sheaf
Above the thousand
Seeds grown wild.

Not my planting,
But by heaven
My harvest —
My own child.

LITTLE SPIRIT TO CHILDLESS COUPLE

Just helping you, Mom and Dad, to develop
A trait you'll need to survive:
Patience – I guarantee you'll need it
Once I arrive.

TO THOSE WHO ASK,
"WHY DOESN'T THE CHURCH
GET INVOLVED IN THE REAL MORAL
AND SOCIAL ISSUES?"

Some gardeners
Slash frantically
At the weed's
Offending shoots —

And others
Labor steadily,
Loosening
Its roots.

AFFIRMATION

Some
Heaven-sought answers
Come in sound —
A voice, perhaps.
But I have found
Mine always come
In utter silence.

My heart,
A swollen sea,
Stops tearing
At its shores
And gradually stills.

The whipping
Of the wind,
The gull's sharp cry —
All sounds
Cease.

I listen
To the answer.

Silence
Speaks clearly:
It speaks peace.

THE USES OF PRAYER

Heaven
Holds out the blessing
Like a bright
Ripe fruit,
Only waiting
For us to ask it:

Our words
Weave the basket.

TO ONE WHO
PRAYS FOR A SIGN

Heaven
Will not open
Out of season,
However we plead.

She knows
The doubtful benefit
Of torrent
To a rootless seed.

PROOF

Proof
Is not the need
Of this unbelieving world.

Though Christ Himself
Comes in evidence,
There will be many
On that day
Whose knee will bow,
Tongue will confess,
And heart
Will turn away.

TO AN ATHEIST

God must have a huge sense of humor
So righteously to resist
The temptation of turning the tables
On your pretending He does not exist.

MARTYR'S PRAYER

Dear God,
I would not turn
From the test of fire.
No flame burns
So hot that
I would leave Thee.

But often,
At weary bedtime,
I cannot hold
My knees to the floor —
So cold,
So very cold.

THE SHEEP

Secure in company,
Watching whosever wool
Happens to be
Up front,

The sheep gladly
Gathers his legs,
And
With blissful "baa"
And unsuspicious sniff,
Dives off
The cliff.

PRACTICE MAKES PERFECT

I'll know better next time
Than to even begin:
Everything's easier on the second try —
Especially sin.

SLIGHT DECEPTION

An adjustable lens is best
For seeing sin:
To soften the view when looking out,
To sharpen it when looking in.

TO ONE WHO HAS
BEEN DONE DIRT

Cry or curse or call it unfair,
But be grateful 'til the grave
That in this hurt
You're the one who received,
And not the one who gave.

TO BE REPEATED ALOUD
ON A DISCOURAGING DAY

God,
The perfect appraiser,
Passed His creatures
In review,
And called each good —
Including you.

THE HEALING

A bird
Once broken
Can never fly,
They say,
Quite so high
Again.

Perhaps.

But as for me,
Now desperately
In need of mending,
I have a healer
Who would restore
These foolish wings
Without a scar.

I will lie quiet
Beneath His touch.
I will listen
As He whispers,
"Rise,
And fall no more."

And then —
Then I shall
Soar.

THE BLOSSOMING

You came
To my garden,
Hungry for beauty
And bold.

I,
Poor, scant bush,
Felt my sap
Turn cold.

Trembling
I gave
One small bud,
And grew back —
Two.

Oh, bless
Nature's cleverness,
Speeding growth
As we consume.

If your hunger
Thrives,
So perhaps
Will my bloom.

HALF-LOVE

Love beyond
The mortal me.
Oh, love the whole.

Look —
This body
(In God's own plan)
Is only half
My soul.

THE HEIGHTS

I have seen
Your heights.
I have walked them —
Up where air is sky,
And a blue breath
Fills and lifts
Toward a farther
Star.

I have walked
The low places
Too —
Down where
The unbeautiful
Has washed,
And breath is heavy
With earth.

I have walked both.
But my eyes choose
To rise
And my feet to climb.

Heights are lovely.
Seek mine.

THE BEST SECURITY

I know
You love me.
But human charms
May wear thin.
And the gold
That holds
A circle
Around your finger
Slips easily,
Even from
The strongest hand.

Yet,
Humbly I rest
In the best
Security:
That white day
We touched in covenant,
Christ came
And widened our wedding
To three.

You
Will be true —
To me,
With good, mortal love —
To Him,
With heaven-hungered
Fidelity.

SHADOWS

My sky has never known
As bright a sun
As you.

I didn't used
To notice clouds a lot,
But now I do.

It's your own
Warm fault
That a simple shadow
Makes cold here.

Please —
Help me find a way
To keep the spaces
Clear.

THE WASTE

They're dumping wheat
Into the sea,
And oranges too,
I hear.

Just like my heart
That annually
Wastes fields of love
For fear.

APART

There have been
Spaces
In our touching —
Distances
Denying
Our embrace.

But somehow
We have grown
Beyond the gulfs,
And now stand
One —
Intimate,
Serene,
Despite
The feeble fact
Of miles
Between.

THE NIGHT

Grief
Is a narrow thing,
Tight against
My breath —
Begging an answer
To unanswerable
Death.

I'm remembering
A sunrise.
I saw the bright
Quick streams of light
Sing gold across
The sky.
And it came to me then
How essential
Is the night:
For only from dark
Do we know dawn
At all.

The memory lets
One small solace in.
If we must
Endure an end
To know the endless —
Oh, gladly
I will let you go:
That when I see you
Standing at the door
To that more
Permanent place,

How quickly
I'll recognize
The eternal
In your embrace.

BETHLEHEM

My pilgrimage to Bethlehem
Was by bus.
I shared my seat
With a crate of irreverent hens
And breathed air bruised by Eastern cigarettes.
I envied the clean, green walk of the shepherds.

At bus stop I looked
For the familiar village of my books.
Boys with toy rifles ran
From little yellowed houses
Up rocky hills playing kill the Jews.

"Guide?" asked a man
At the Church of the Nativity.
"Thank you, no, I can't pay a guide."
"No charge. Please. Is free."

He showed me the place
Where they say the birth was,
Down underneath the stairs.
I breathed for hay
And listened for the lambs.
But the sputtering of perfumed wax
Got in my way —
And the Latin chanting from the church above —
And my guide proudly pointing out
Which sect owned which part
Of the ornamented, golden altar.
"Beautiful, no?"
"Yes. Lovely."

We stepped out of the church
Into his small shop.
"Here you buy souvenir of Bethlehem.
Very nice. Very cheap."

Waiting for the bus to leave
I fingered my small New Testament
With its carved cover
And my two salad sets of olive wood.
The boys ran by with their rifles
And a radio rocked out The Beatles.

Oh, Bethlehem was better in my dreams.

The sky was darkening when the bus
Lurched its return to the city.

There — above the hill — one star,
One tiny, bright, honest-to-heaven star.
I turned the pages of my new souvenir.

Heaven and earth shall pass away . . .
But I am the same,
Yesterday, today, and forever.

I leaned back, listened to the lambs,
And smelled the hay.

STANDING BEFORE THE GREAT PYRAMID

I will be interested at judgment day
To hear Cheops defend
The sum of human souls that was sucked
To build this pile of sand.

WORDS

I wanted to know
What it felt like to swear.

So one day —
Away out in the back pasture where
Two horses switched
For the big flies —
I stood on a little bridge,
Took a deep breath,
And said every bad word
I'd ever heard.

The horses' tails switched on,
And on ran the unpolluted stream.

It took about a week, though,
To wash and rinse
My mouth clean,
And I've never said those words since —

Though now I'm counting
Many another word
I should have taken
To where only horses heard.

FOR THE FRIENDLY
NEIGHBORHOOD GOSSIP

The children's turtle
Stayed in his shell
One day.
He's sick,
They thought.
And to see
If the poor thing
Was still alive
They got some sticks
To poke inside.

They were right.
Pretty soon
Poor turtle
Died.

INDEPENDENCE

I would stay here —
Close to roots
That fed me —
Close to
Cool shelter —

Always close
I would be.

Except,
I'm afraid.

Have you seen
The pitiful
Small green
That grows
In shade?

THE INHERITANCE

At the funeral my friend said to me,
"What hurts most is that
Mother was always sad.
I think now
A mother owes it to her children
Just to be happy.
She never was."

Her sad face
Looked at the sad face backed by velvet.

Last time I saw my friend,
Now a year since,
The eyes were dry,
But the face was pinched
As then, and anxious hands worked
The buttons of her little girl's coat.

"I can't stay."
(She never did.)
"Jim's working tonight — as always —
But at last he got a raise.
Won't go far with the baby coming, though,
And we'll have to find a bigger place.
So tired and depressed all the time.
I don't know —
Guess we'll manage —
But kids seem to need so much."

We talked a while.
Then —
"Have to go — so much to do."
I watched her rise,
And do the buttons of their coats,
And sigh.

A little wide-eyed girl watched, too.

THE GRACIOUS HOST

The sins of the fathers,
He knew,
Shall visit the children.

And when his
Came knocking,
He opened the door,
Swept the best bedroom,
And fed them from his table
Three times a day.

Before long
His guests decided
To stay.

PROTECTION

Take my hand,
Child:
There are dangers
At our feet.

I grope
The uneven ground
Through mist,
Fearfully and slow.
But you —
(Oh, take my hand)
You go
With unsuspicious eyes,
With trusting walk.

There are dangers
At our feet,
And I see them all.

Take my hand,
Child —
Lest I fall.

OF FATE AND
THE FIRE DEPARTMENT

Can't
Get around prophecy,
Said Mister Amen.

So under the bed
He hid,
Cursing fate
While he fried —

All because
A friend had
Phoned in concern
To tell him that
His roof was aflame
And his house
About to burn.

IN DEFENSE OF SMILING
DESPITE THE HEADLINES

Are there not
Two sides
To the duty
A man owes
The sad world
He rides
A moment here? —

To decrease a bit
The measure
Of misery,
And
To increase a bit
The measure
Of cheer.

COMPENSATION

Enormous grief
Has leveled me —
Welded its bulk
To my back
And will not let
Me rise.

Yet —
"I'll give
No burden that
You cannot bear,"
He promised me.

I am amazed —
How strong my back
Must be.

OLD AGE

No summit,
This mountain top —

Just
A pleasant place
To straighten the back,
Take a clean breath,
Survey the view
That suddenly
Is so vast —

Just
A quick rest,
And then —
Upward again.